CSPE Activity Book

Stand Up, Speak Up!

Hugh Holmes
Gearoidín O'Dwyer

MENTOR BOOKS

MENTOR BOOKS

43 Furze Road
Sandyford Industrial Estate
Dublin 18
Tel: 01-2952112
Fax: 01-2952114
Website: www.mentorbooks.ie
e-mail: admin@mentorbooks.ie

Edited by:
Una Whelan

Cover Design & Layout:
Mary Byrne

Cover photograph: Jupiter Images Unlimited

Illustrations:
Peter Donnelly, Jupiter Images Unlimited

ISBN: 978-1-906623-45-6

© Hugh Holmes & Gearoidín O'Dwyer 2010

9 10 8

Paper Statement
The paper used in this book is made from the wood pulp of managed forests.
For every tree felled, at least one tree is planted, thereby renewing natural resources.

Contents

ACKNOWLEDGEMENTS

Jupiter Images Unlimited; Getty Images; Pluto Press: extract from *50 Reasons to Buy Fair Trade* by Miles Litvinoff and John Madeley; *The Meath Chronicle*; *The Irish Times*; *Irish Independent*; S.A.E.N. (Stop Animal Exploitation Now); Pavee Point; Concern; Bóthar; Trócaire; Focus Ireland; Goal; Martyn Turner; Niall Mellon Township Trust; An Garda Síochána; The Fairtrade Foundation.

The Publishers have made every effort to trace and acknowledge the holders of copyright material used in this book. In the event of any copyright holder having been omitted, the Publishers will come to a suitable agreement at the first opportunity.

INTRODUCTION

Activity 1 - Fill in the Gaps

Welcome to your new subject **C** _____ **S** _____ and **P** _____
E _____. Over the next three years you are going to learn about becoming an
Active **C** _____ and making a difference to the community at home and abroad.

This course is based around seven concepts: Human Dignity, **R** _____ and
Responsibilities, **S** _____, Democracy, Development, **L** _____ and
Interdependence.

We hope you enjoy learning more about the world around you and how you can
make it a better place.

Activity 2 - Questionnaire

**Are you a good citizen? Tick your answer below and add up your score to
see how good a citizen you are.**

1   **I always put my rubbish in the bin.**
    Yes (5) ❑   Sometimes (3) ❑   No (0) ❑

2   **I never graffiti other people's property.**
    Yes (5) ❑   Sometimes (3) ❑   No (0) ❑

3   **I watch the news and read newspapers.**
    Yes (5) ❑   Sometimes (3) ❑   No (0) ❑

4   **I follow the school rules.**
    Yes (5) ❑   Sometimes (3) ❑   No (0) ❑

5   **I recycle when I can.**
    Yes (5) ❑   Sometimes (3) ❑   No (0) ❑

6   **I play my music as loud as I want without thinking of others.**
    Yes (0) ❑   Sometimes (3) ❑   No (5) ❑

7   **I always turn off lights when I leave a room.**
    Yes (5) ❑   Sometimes (3) ❑   No (0) ❑

8   **I buy Fairtrade products when I can.**
    Yes (5) ❑   Sometimes (3) ❑   No (0) ❑

9   **I'm quiet in class so that others can learn.**
    Yes (5) ❑   Sometimes (3) ❑   No (0) ❑

10 **I never visit older relatives or neighbours.**
    Yes (0) ❑   Sometimes (3) ❑   No (5) ❑

Score

How did you do?
0 - 19
A lot of work to do but by taking part
in CSPE you can change this
20 - 34
Not bad but still some work to do
35 - 50
You are on your way to being a
model citizen

Activity 3 – Word Search

Find the following words in the word search:

CITIZEN – COMMUNITY – DEMOCRACY – DEVELOPMENT – HUMAN DIGNITY
INDIVIDUAL – INTERDEPENDENCE – LAW – STATE – STEWARDSHIP – WORLD

```
I  P  L  U  I  Z  I  Q  X  Y  K  Y  H  W  A
W  N  S  A  O  S  W  V  C  R  N  T  U  O  V
S  Y  T  H  U  F  T  A  S  U  L  I  M  R  O
F  T  E  E  L  D  R  A  U  P  D  N  A  L  S
I  O  V  A  R  C  I  M  T  E  Y  U  N  D  B
Q  Q  W  A  O  D  P  V  V  E  X  M  D  J  J
B  E  Y  M  X  C  E  E  I  L  B  M  I  Y  X
I  S  E  E  Z  J  L  P  E  D  H  O  G  I  O
H  D  L  W  E  O  W  O  E  B  N  C  N  Y  Q
E  U  I  C  P  F  M  A  Y  N  I  I  I  O  V
K  G  A  M  X  D  Q  J  T  F  D  V  T  S  B
J  G  E  F  N  L  T  Q  U  J  H  E  Y  J  U
Y  N  Z  L  C  I  T  I  Z  E  N  N  N  F  E
T  P  I  H  S  D  R  A  W  E  T  S  A  C  P
Z  B  X  N  P  G  P  Z  W  T  I  I  M  F  E
```

Activity 4 – Match 'Em Up

Match the CSPE concepts A-G with their meanings 1-7. Use each concept only once.

Meaning	Course Concept
1 Caring responsibly for our environment and the planet on which we live ☐	**A.** Human Dignity
2 Government by the people, through voting and elections ☐	**B.** Rights and Responsibilities
3 Improvements taking place in communities at home and abroad ☐	**C.** Democracy
4 The ways in which we are connected with other individuals and communities around the globe ☐	**D.** Law
5 When every person is respected, and has their basic needs met, allowing them to reach their full potential ☐	**E.** Interdependence
6 The recognition of the right of every citizen around the world to have their basic needs met ☐	**F.** Development
7 The creation and running of a just, fair and safe society ☐	**G.** Stewardship

Adapted from Junior Certificate Exam

Activity 5 - Answer the Questions

Read the article below and answer the questions that follow.

Being a good citizen means using your own talents and interests to make a positive difference for others in the world, near or far. Read the story below of how Chelsea striker, Didier Drogba, has used his love of soccer and his success in life to help the people of his native country.

Didier Drogba Foundation

Chelsea striker Didier Drogba was born in the west African country, Ivory Coast. In the early 1980s the country was plunged into poverty due to falling prices for their main exports, cocoa and coffee. Drogba's parents found themselves under huge financial pressure and when Drogba was five, they made the heartbreaking decision to send their son to live with his uncle in France. They hoped that this would give him the opportunity of a better education and life.

With nobody to accompany him, the five-year-old Drogba cried all the way during the six-hour flight. Three years later, suffering from homesickness, Drogba went home, but once again had to leave as neither of his parents had work.

Didier Drogba, who learned his soccer skills in a dusty car park in his home city of Abidjan, is today a millionaire sportsman. Known in almost every country in the world, he is the most famous person ever born in Ivory Coast. However, he has never forgotten the poverty of his childhood.

These days, despite his fame and fortune, he has more than soccer on his mind. On a recent trip home, he was shocked and humbled by the poverty of the children and the lack of a proper hospital for the community. As a result, he set up the Didier Drogba Foundation to provide financial support in health and education for the African people. His first major project is to build and fund a hospital in his home city 'to give people basic healthcare and a chance to stay alive'.

Drogba asked for his £3 million sponsorship fee from his first ever Pepsi ad to be used to help build the new hospital. 'To open the hospital would be the best achievement of my life. That would be my contribution to Ivory Coast. The minimum I can do is to make them feel important,' Drogba said recently. 'I am lucky enough to have made a career out of my passion and now it is my turn to return the favour.'

1 What caused the poverty in Ivory Coast in the 1980s which forced Didier Drogba's parents to send him to France?

_____

_____

_____

_____

2 How has Didier Drogba used his talent for football to become an active citizen, helping the people of his native country?

_____

_____

_____

_____

_____

3 Write a brief account of any other active citizen you know, famous or not, who has helped make the world a better place.

_____

_____

_____

_____

_____

_____

_____

_____

_____

_____

Activity 6 – Picture Perfect

In the space below, design a poster encouraging young people to become Active Citizens. Think about your own talents and interests. Don't forget to use colouring pencils or markers.

Activity 6 – Picture Perfect

CONCEPT 1 Human Diginity

Activity 1 – Get Writing

Explain what you understand by each of the following ideas:

Human Dignity

_____

_____

_____

Stereotype

_____

_____

_____

Discrimination

_____

_____

_____

Activity 2 – Word Search

Find the following words in the word search:
TRAVELLERS – EQUALITY – DISCRIMINATION – RACISM – HOMELESSNESS,
STEREOTYPE – BULLYING – NEEDS – MULTICULTURAL – RESPECT

```
D  U  E  O  W  L  V  G  N  P  J  Y  V  M  Y
S  I  B  P  W  F  K  S  B  O  U  N  B  U  T
R  J  S  E  Y  A  S  B  G  V  M  L  E  L  I
N  A  Y  C  Q  T  T  F  F  A  O  L  H  T  L
E  Y  C  V  R  D  O  T  A  Y  D  O  D  I  A
E  Y  C  I  G  I  H  E  I  R  M  K  F  C  U
D  R  P  B  S  I  M  G  R  E  H  U  T  U  Q
S  I  I  D  T  M  Q  I  L  E  G  W  P  L  E
O  Z  Q  A  J  J  A  E  N  N  T  F  Q  T  C
P  T  O  C  O  Z  S  U  I  A  Y  S  T  U  L
N  N  U  K  V  S  J  Y  J  R  T  A  A  R  C
U  L  W  C  N  C  L  R  B  L  Q  I  M  A  O
J  S  R  E  L  L  E  V  A  R  T  T  O  L  P
V  Y  S  I  U  R  E  S  P  E  C  T  K  N  I
Z  S  W  B  X  P  F  K  Z  K  O  B  B  G  Y
```

Activity 3 – Answer the Questions: Homelessness

Read the following accounts of homelessness and answer the questions.

Derek (17)

'We lost our home when I was twelve because my parents split up and my mother had no job. I didn't know what was going on; I thought we were just moving to a different place. The next thing I knew we were living on the streets. I was confused and worried about what was going to happen to us. I remember being scared that someone was going to hurt or even kill us. For a while we ended up sleeping in our car and then Mam thought we'd have a better chance in England with my aunty.

Things were no better there. Mam still couldn't get work and my aunty didn't have enough room for us to stay for long. So we ended up back in Ireland on the streets in Sligo. We used to get €34 a week to live on. We were starving – we'd rob stuff and everything just to feed ourselves. Once, all my clothes and shoes were robbed. I never touched drugs. Other people did, but I never did. We used to be filthy – our clothes were in bits from sleeping out. I felt other people were looking down on us.'

Derek went to Focus Ireland drop-in centre for young people and is now settled in a home of his own.

Rosie (15) and Jack (1)

'He was only three days old. I wanted to keep him but I had been kicked out of home when my parents found out I was pregnant. I moved into a hostel but it wasn't a good place to bring up a baby. It was scary for me and Jack. When Jack used to cry, some of the other women would shout at us and then Jack cried even louder. I had nowhere to go and no one to help me.

One day I met a social worker who sent me to Focus Ireland's mother and baby unit. I was only supposed to stay there for three weeks but I didn't want to leave. We felt safe there and it was lovely and clean. They showed me how to look after Jack.'

Happily, Rosie and Jack are now living in Focus Ireland's long-term housing, where Jack is preparing for school.

1 Derek says, 'I felt other people were looking down on us.' Why does Derek think this?

_____

_____

_____

_____

2 Name some of the difficulties Derek faced while living on the streets.

_____

_____

_____

_____

3 Why did Rosie become homeless?

_____

_____

_____

_____

4 How did Focus Ireland help Rosie and Jack?

_____

_____

_____

_____

5 What do you think is the most difficult aspect of being homeless?

_____

_____

_____

_____

_____

_____

Activity 4 – Answer the Questions: Homelessness

1 Name **THREE** organisations that help homeless people in Ireland.

(a) _____

(b) _____

(c) _____

2 Give **TWO** reasons why a person may become homeless.

(a) _____

(b) _____

3 Describe the possible effects of homelessness on a person.

_____

_____

_____

_____

4 Describe **ONE** action your CSPE class could take to raise awareness about the issue of homelessness.

_____

_____

_____

_____

_____

Activity 5 – Get Writing: A Poem about Bullying

Read the poem below and imagine you are 'The Loner'. Write a diary entry for one day in your life. Try to capture your feelings and anxieties about school. Explain how you would like life to be.

The Loner by *Julie Holder*

He leans against the playground wall,
Smacks his hands against the bricks
And other boredom-beating tricks,
Traces patterns with his feet.
Scuffs to make the tarmac squeak,
Back against the wall he stays
And never plays.

The playground's quick with life,
The beat is strong.
Though sharp as a knife
Strife doesn't last long.
There is shouting, laughter, song,
And a place at the wall
For who won't belong.

We pass him running, skipping, walking,
In slow huddled groups, low talking.
Each in our familiar clique
We pass him by and never speak,
His loneliness is his shell and shield
And neither he nor we will yield.
He wasn't there at the wall today,
Someone said he'd moved away
To another school and place
And on the wall where he used to lean
Someone had chalked 'watch this space'.

Diary entry: _____
_____
_____
_____
_____
_____
_____
_____
_____
_____
_____
_____
_____
_____

Activity 6 – Answer the Questions: Discrimination

Read the article below and answer the questions that follow:

Woman (74) wins age-bias case

A seventy-four-year-old woman who has won an age discrimination case against Ulster Bank has encouraged all older people to challenge discrimination when they encounter it.

Phyllis Fahey from Rathfarnham, Dublin, was refused a car loan from Ulster Bank's Maynooth branch when she was seventy years of age, although she had been a customer at the branch for ten years. She had no other borrowings with Ulster Bank and both her and her husband's pensions were paid directly into the Maynooth branch.

She said a bank official told her it was bank policy not to grant loans to anybody over the age of sixty-five. The official was apologetic, but said that those were the bank's rules.

The Equality Tribunal found she had been discriminated against because of her age and ordered the bank to pay her €2,000 in compensation for the upset and humiliation experienced. An Ulster Bank spokesman said the bank was disappointed with the outcome of the case, 'Ulster Bank would like to confirm that there was no upper age limit in relation to applications for a personal loan.'

Ms. Fahey's victory was described by the Equality Authority as 'hugely significant.' Ms. Fahey herself said she was 'very proud' of the victory, 'I was very nervous taking on the bank. It took me three-and-a-half years but I just went in there and told the truth. Banks are just people after all.'

She said she saw discrimination against older people every day of the week. 'This is happening in every walk of life and I would say to people, "don't be afraid. Take them on." The lack of humanity towards older people, particularly people in care, is appalling.

She later got a car loan from the credit union. 'They said to me "How much do you want?" and gave me a voucher for petrol,' she recalled.

Age Action also welcomed the victory and said older people with good credit records were frequently refused loans by banks. 'Today's ruling means another obstacle has been removed for older people,' Eamon Timmins, Age Action spokesman said.

Adapted from an article by Alison Healy, published in The Irish Times

1 Why was Ms. Fahey refused the car loan?

_____

_____

2 What is the term for this type of discrimination?

_____

3 Ms. Fahey talks about the lack of humanity towards older people. Give **ONE** example of older people who she says are not treated well.

_____

4 Name **ONE** organisation which protects the rights of older people.

_____

5 Name **TWO** other types of discrimination.

(a) _____

(b) _____

Activity 7 – Answer the Questions: Disability

Read the article below and answer the questions that follow.

Disabled Student Sues Store for Discrimination

Riam Dean was just days into a part-time job at Abercrombie & Fitch's London store when she says she was asked to leave the shop floor because she broke the company's 'Look Policy'.

Riam was born without her left forearm and has worn a prosthetic (artificial) limb since she was three months old. She says she never allowed her disability to get in her way.

She applied for a job with the company to fund the final months of her law degree. She says that when she told A&F about her disability after getting the job, the firm agreed that she could wear a white cardigan to cover her arm. Shortly afterwards, however, a worker from the 'visual team' demanded that she take the cardigan off. A few minutes later, according to Riam, her manager came over to her and said, 'I can't have you on the shop floor as you are breaking the Look Policy. Go to the stockroom immediately and I'll get someone to replace you.' Riam said, 'I pride myself on being quite a confident girl but I had never experienced prejudice like that before and it made me feel utterly worthless.'

Four years ago Abercrombie settled a €25 million lawsuit in which nine former employees accused the firm of discrimination. The people, all from ethnic minority groups, said they were forced to work in stockrooms or take night shifts because they did not fit the 'Abercrombie look.'

A spokesman for the company said, 'A&F has a strong anti-discrimination policy and is committed to providing a supportive and dignified environment for all of its employees.'

However, Riam said that she had worked for twenty years to build up her 'personal confidence' and that she was 'much more than a girl with only one arm.' She said the event 'made me question my worth as a human being.'

1 According to Riam, how was she discriminated against?

_____

_____

_____

2 How did this make her feel?

_____

_____

_____

3 What other type of discrimination is mentioned in the article?

_____

4 If this occurred in Ireland what law would protect Riam's rights?

_____

Activity 8 – Exam Practice: Traveller Culture

Pavee's Ireland

International day
against racism
21st March

DRAMA

EDUCATION

POLITICAL

MUSIC

SPORTS

ACTIVISM

"Human rights are not negotiable
so the price that people sometimes
have to pay to protect them is
never too high"
Thomas McCann, Traveller rights activist

These are some of the Travellers who have contributed to Irish society

Mickey Dunne, piper, pipe maker
Pecker Dunne, musician
Keenan Family, John (father)
Johnny, Paddy and **Brendan**
Furey Family, Ted (father)

Eddie, Finbar, Paul and **George**
Margaret Barry, singer
Cathy Maguire, singer
John Doherty, fiddler
Jemmy Byrne, piper
Felix Doran, piper
John Cash, piper

Collins Family, tin whistle, accordion
Tom Stokes, Longford councillor
Ellen Morgan, Mayo councillor
Martin Ward, Galway councillor
Martin Collins,

Human Rights Commissioner
Frankie Barrett, boxer, Olympic
Anthony McDonagh, power lifter Galway
Michael Collins, actor
Declan Joyce, scriptwriter US

Rosaleen McDonagh, playwright
Catherine Joyce
Nan Joyce
Thomas McCann
Chrissie Ward

Davey Joyce
Maureen Ward
Marie Joyce
Chrissie Sullivan
Michael McDonagh
Winnie McDonagh

and there are many more

Published by Pavee Point Travellers Centre, North Great Charles Street, Dublin 1. Telephone: 01 878 0255

Pavee's Ireland

When you have studied the poster, answer the questions below.

1 What event was celebrated on 21 March?

_____

_____

From the poster, select **TWO** different areas of Irish life in which the Travelling Community is involved.

First Area _____

Second Area _____

(3 marks)

2 Where is the Pavee Point Travellers Centre?

_____

_____

According to Thomas McCann, why is the price that people have to pay to protect human rights never too high?

_____

_____

(3 marks)

3 Travellers have a separate and different culture to settled people. Describe **TWO** ways Traveller culture is different to the culture of settled people.

First Way _____

_____

Second Way _____

_____

(4 marks)

4 Describe **TWO** actions that **YOU** and **YOUR CSPE CLASS** could take to celebrate the Travelling Community.

First Action _____

Second Action _____

(4 marks)

Adapted from Junior Certificate Exam

Activity 9 – Exam Practice: Traveller Discrimination

The Irish Traveller Movement conducted a survey among Travellers recording the types of discrimination that Travellers experience when looking for service in shops, hotels and pubs. The following information highlights the results of this survey. Study the information and answer the questions that follow.

Pubs 88% of Travellers said they went to a pub.	Of this 88%, 77% said they had been told to leave a pub by bar staff.	79% of Travellers who went to a pub said they had been refused a drink.	71% of these said they had been refused 'because we were Travellers'.
Hotels 61% said they had tried to book a hotel for an occasion.	Of this 61%, 76% said they had experienced problems.	47% of Travellers who had experienced difficulties said that it was 'because we were Travellers'.	45% of Travellers who had tried to book a hotel for an occasion said they were asked to leave or cancel their booking.
Shops 54% of Travellers said they had been asked to leave a shop.	66% said they had experienced others being served before them.	60% said they had been 'made a show of' (embarrassed) in shops.	

1 What percentage of Travellers who went to a pub said they had been refused a drink?

_____

(2 marks)

2 What percentage of Travellers said they had tried to book a hotel for an occasion?

_____

(2 marks)

3 What percentage of Travellers said they had experienced others being served before them in shops?_____

(2 marks)

4 From this survey name **ONE** human right that some Travellers may have been denied?

_____

(2 marks)

5 Travellers have a separate and different culture from settled people. Describe **TWO** ways that Traveller culture is different from the culture of settled people. Your answer must be written from a human rights approach.

(a) _____

_____

(b) _____

_____

(4 marks)

6 Apart from Travellers, can you name a group of people who may have experienced discrimination? Describe how these people have been discriminated against, and then suggest **TWO** ways that this type of discrimination could be prevented?

Name of the group _____

(2 marks)

How they may have experienced discrimination

_____

_____

(2 marks)

Two ways to prevent this type of discrimination

(a) _____

_____

_____

(b) _____

_____

_____

(4 marks)

Adapted from Junior Certificate Exam

Activity 10 - Picture Perfect: Racism

Design a poster to celebrate International Day Against Racism, 21 March.

CONCEPT 2 Rights and Responsibilities

Activity 1 - Get Writing!

Explain each of the following:

Human Rights

_____

_____

_____

_____

Responsibilities

_____

_____

_____

_____

Universal Declaration of Human Rights (UDHR)

_____

_____

_____

_____

Activity 2 - Fill in the Gaps: Human Rights

1 The **U** _____ **D** _____ of Human Rights was signed in 1948 in order to protect human rights around the world.

2 There are 30 **A** _____ in the UDHR.

3 On 10 December we celebrate **I**_____ **H** _____
   R _____ Day.

4 **A** _____ **I** _____ is an organisation which works to end human rights abuses around the world, particularly the death penalty.

Activity 3 – Match 'Em Up: Human Rights

Look at the rights 1-10 below and match them to the correct pictures A-J.

1   The right to marry.
2   The right to work.
3   The right to a fair trial.
4   The right to freedom of expression.
5   The right to vote.
6   The right to medical treatment.
7   The right to rest and leisure.
8   The right to own property.
9   The right to freedom from slavery.
10 The right to protest.

1 =	3 =	5 =	7 =	9 =
2 =	4 =	6 =	8 =	10 =

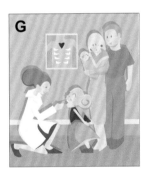

Activity 4 – Picture Perfect: Rights

In the spaces below, draw pictures to represent the following rights:

THE RIGHT TO EDUCATION

THE RIGHT TO PRACTISE A RELIGION OF YOUR CHOICE

THE RIGHT TO TRAVEL

Activity 5 - Answer the Questions: UDHR

Read the article below and answer the questions that follow.
Human rights: **Each of us has a role to play.**

Mary Robinson, former UN High Commissioner for Human Rights, talks about the role of the individual in protecting human rights.

Every single person has a role to play when it comes to human rights. No one person, no matter what position they hold, can ignore this. As UN High Commissioner for Human Rights I had special responsibility to protect and promote human rights. It was a difficult job but very worthwhile.

This is a very troubled world and we are a long way from achieving the goals of the Universal Declaration of Human Rights for millions of people worldwide. I hope that by examining the UDHR and human rights abuses throughout the world, you will see your own responsibility and how you can fulfil it.

Poverty affects human rights in almost every country, including Ireland. Every year 13 to 18 million people, mainly women and children, die from hunger or hunger-related causes. That's 35,000 a day – or 1,500 an hour. While you are in one short class period, more than 750 children will die from the effects of hunger. It's the same as two jumbo jets crashing with no survivors, every half hour of every day. Can we stop it? Can we let it continue? Have we a responsibility?

I was proud to stand beside former President Nelson Mandela in South Africa to launch the fiftieth anniversary year of the Universal Declaration of Human Rights in 1997. Perhaps more than any other leader, he understands the importance of human rights and the dignity of the individual.

On 10 December each year we remember the adoption of the UDHR and honour human rights defenders from all over the world. But we have little reason to celebrate. Now, more than sixty years after the declaration was adopted, countless millions are still denied their human rights.

I hope that all of you become human rights defenders so that future generations will be able to celebrate the declaration. Let us commit ourselves to converting the words of the declaration to reality for the millions of people who desperately need it.

Adapted from the Irish Independent

1   What position did Mary Robinson hold with the United Nations, and what special responsibility did she have?

_____

_____

2   What threatens human rights' around the world, according to Mary Robinson?

_____

_____

3   What other human rights defender is mentioned in the article?

_____

4   Why does Mary Robinson think we have little to celebrate In relation to the Universal Declaration of Human Rights?

_____

_____

_____

_____

5   *'Let us commit ourselves to converting the words of the Declaration to reality for the millions of people who desperately need it.'* What do you think Mary Robinson means by this statement?

_____

_____

_____

_____

Activity 6 – Answer the Questions: Human Rights

1   Name **THREE** organisations that work to secure people's human rights.

   (a) _____

   (b) _____

   (c) _____

2   Write down **TWO** actions your **CSPE** class could take to protect human rights.

   (a) _____

   (b) _____

3   Name **THREE** places where people's rights are denied today and explain the reasons for this.

   (a) _____

   _____

   (b) _____

   _____

   (c) _____

   _____

Activity 7 – Get Writing: Citizens' Responsibilities

Imagine you work for the United Nations. You have been asked to draw up a Declaration of Responsibilities. Think about responsibilities for the individual, the community, the nation and the world. Write this below.

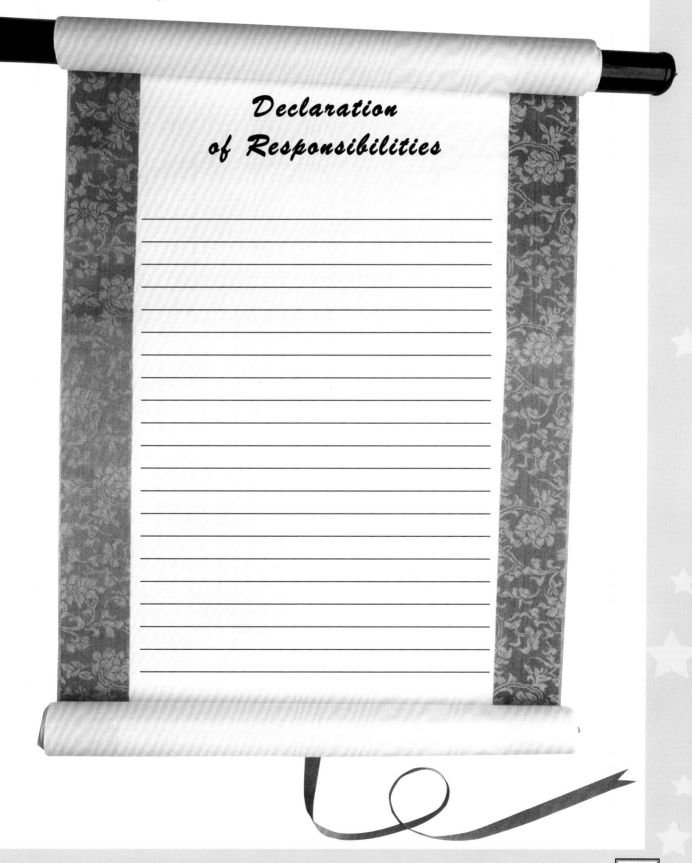

Declaration of Responsibilities

Activity 8 – Picture Perfect: Human Rights Activists

**Go online or search newspapers for human rights activists.
In the spaces below insert THREE pictures of human rights activists from
Ireland or around the world.**

Name _____

Name _____   Name _____

Activity 9 – Picture Perfect: Amnesty International

Reflecting upon the quotation *'The pen is mightier than the sword'* design a poster for your school to advertise the work of Amnesty International. Include the Amnesty logo and focus particularly on Amnesty's letter-writing campaigns.

Activity 10 – Exam Practice: Child Labour

Study the poster below and answer the questions that follow.

Child labour involves children in the making of bricks, working with machinery in agriculture and carpet weaving, in domestic labour, in the sex industry, in construction work, in deep-sea fishing and in the making of matches and fireworks and hundreds of other activities that deny children the right to full-time education.

1 Child labour denies children the right to what? _____
How many young people between the ages of five and seventeen are defined as child labourers? _____
What is the website address for this campaign to stop child labour?
_____
(3 marks)

2 Name **THREE** different types of work in which child labourers are involved.
First type _____
Second type _____
Third type _____
(3 marks)

3 The Protection of Young Persons (Employment) Act, 1996 states that the maximum weekly working hours are 0 hours for fourteen-year-olds and 8 hours for fifteen-year-olds during school term-time and 35 hours per week during holidays. Give **ONE** reason why you think this law was brought in.
_____
_____
_____
(2 marks)

4 The International Labour Organisation estimates that 246 million children between the ages of five and seventeen years of age are working as child labourers. Most of these children are in Asia (60%) and in Africa (32%).
Suggest **ONE** action **THE IRISH GOVERNMENT** could take to help reduce the number of child labourers.
_____
_____
_____
_____
(2 marks)

5 As a citizen of Ireland you also can play a role. Suggest **TWO** actions **YOU** could take to inform people in your community about child labour.
First action _____
_____
_____
_____

Second action _____
_____
_____
_____
(4 marks)

Adapted from Junior Certificate Exam

Activity 11 – Answer the Questions: Animal Welfare

Study the Animal Rights poster below and answer the questions that follow.

1 Name **ONE** organisation that supports this protest.

_____

2 How can you contact the organisation?

_____

3 According to the poster, what are animals being used for?

_____

_____

4 What are the protestors demanding?

_____

_____

5 Name **TWO** actions your **CSPE** class could undertake to create awareness of animal rights and welfare.

First action _____

_____

_____

_____

Second action _____

_____

_____

_____

Activity 12 - Crossword

Across
  2. The Universal _____ of Human Rights was established in 1948 (11)
  3. This International group use letter writing to protect rights of prisoners (7)
  7. The _____ for Children looks after the interests of children in Ireland (9)

Down
  1. The practice of experimenting on live animals (11)
  4. The Convention on the Rights of the _____ lists special rights for young people (5)
  5. Human rights activist who campaigned for the people of East Timor.
     Hint: First name is 'Tom'. (Refer to your textbook if you need to) (6)
  6. Child _____ is the practice of denying young people a childhood by making them work (6)

CONCEPT 3 Stewardship

Activity 1 – Get Writing!

Explain each of the following:

Stewardship

_____

_____

_____

_____

Global Warming

_____

_____

_____

Carbon Footprint

_____

_____

_____

_____

Activity 2 – Word Search

Find the following words in the word search:
CARBON – CONSERVATION – EARTH – EXTINCTION – GREENPEACE – KYOTO
RECYCLING – SOLAR ENERGY – STEWARDSHIP

H	R	P	F	F	U	V	D	V	G	X	W	E	Y	Y
B	E	E	A	L	E	D	Z	R	M	C	K	P	I	G
B	O	C	V	Y	C	C	X	R	Y	R	S	U	C	R
F	P	J	E	H	V	A	F	X	L	O	P	K	I	E
N	O	I	T	A	V	R	E	S	N	O	C	B	N	N
C	E	M	H	I	I	B	E	Q	U	Q	Y	O	G	E
V	Z	S	Z	S	X	O	I	C	B	V	I	Z	R	R
T	V	Z	V	W	D	N	C	P	Y	T	U	X	K	A
U	H	J	M	E	K	R	L	H	C	C	D	U	V	L
V	N	T	B	E	W	I	A	N	W	A	L	F	B	O
U	K	W	A	R	C	Y	I	W	D	P	S	I	L	S
W	B	R	K	G	G	T	R	K	E	A	S	I	N	R
Q	T	W	C	Y	X	K	C	W	O	T	O	Y	K	G
H	G	R	E	E	N	P	E	A	C	E	S	I	N	F
M	C	T	D	B	C	Q	L	F	P	V	Q	P	U	K	P

Activity 3 - Fill in the Gaps: Global Warming

Look at the section about global warming in your textbook and fill in the gaps below.

Global warming is caused by too much **C** _____ **D** _____ in the atmosphere. This is released when we burn **F** _____ **F** _____. This causes heat to be trapped and the earth to warm up. It is known as the **G**_____ effect.

Global warming will have a devastating effect on the planet. If rainfall is reduced it will cause **D** _____. If plants can't grow and animals can't survive, millions of people will die from **S** _____.

One way of tackling global warming is to reduce your **C** _____ footprint. This can be done by following the code Reduce, **R** _____, **R** _____.

Activity 4 - Answer the Questions: Alternative Energy

1   Nuclear power is a highly controversial energy source. Give **ONE** argument in favour of nuclear power and **ONE** argument against.
    For _____
    _____
    Against _____
    _____

2   Fossil fuels such as coal release a lot of carbon dioxide into the atmosphere when they are burned. Name **THREE** types of alternative energy sources other than nuclear power.
    • _____
    • _____
    • _____

3   What is the Kyoto Protocol?
    _____
    _____

4   Earth Hour is an annual event that encourages people to use less electricity by turning off their lights for one hour. Do you think this is an effective way of tackling global warming? Explain your answer.
    _____
    _____
    _____
    _____
    _____

Activity 5 – Match 'Em Up: Where Will all the Rubbish Go?

Ireland produces 3 million tonnes of rubbish every year. This has to go somewhere but what should we do with it all?

Look at the items below and suggest the most environmentally friendly way of getting rid of the rubbish. Some suggestions have been provided.

Reuse

Wormery

Washing machine

Newspaper

Glass bottles

Tea bags

Return to shop when you're buying a new one

Apple cores

Jeans

Charity Shop

Woollen jumper

Mobile phone

Recycling Bin

Printer cartridges

Cardboard

Compost

Laptop

Sell or give to someone else

Metal cans

Plastic bottles

Books

Charities like the Jack and Jill Foundation

Furniture

Mountain bike

Clothes collection for the Developing World

Any other ideas?

Activity 6 – Picture Perfect: Waste Management

Create a poster as part of a campaign encouraging young people to deal with their waste responsibly. Don't forget to include a slogan and lots of colour.

Activity 7 - Questionnaire: How Environmentally Friendly Are You?

Let's find out if you're an Environmental Slob or an Eco Warrior.
Tick your answers below and then add up your score at the end.

1 Are your school copybooks made from recycled paper?

Yes (5) ❑   Some of them (3) ❑   No (0) ❑

2 Do you leave the tap running when you brush your teeth?

Yes (0) ❑   From time to time (3) ❑   Never (5) ❑

3 Does your family bring bottles to the bottle bank?

Yes (5) ❑   The odd time (3) ❑   No, bottles go out with the rubbish (0) ❑

4 How do you get to school?

By car (0) ❑   By public transport (3) ❑   Walk or cycle (5) ❑

5 Do you leave your TV / stereo / DVD player, etc. on standby?

Yes (0) ❑   Sometimes (3) ❑   I always turn it off fully (5) ❑

6 Do you buy vintage / second-hand clothes?

Yes (5) ❑   Some of the time (3) ❑   No, all my clothes are brand new (0)

7 Do you drop litter on the ground?

Yes (0) ❑   Occasionally (3) ❑   Never (5) ❑

8 Have you ever taken part in a community clean-up or Tidy Towns competition?

More than once (5) ❑   Once (3) ❑   Never (0) ❑

9 When you're boiling the kettle, do you use just the amount of water that you need?

Yes (5) ❑   Sometimes (3) ❑   I always fill it to the top (0) ❑

10 Do you turn out lights when you leave a room?

Yes (5) ❑   Sometimes I forget (3) ❑   I never remember to turn out the light (0) ❑

Score
So, how did you do?

36 – 50
Well done. You are an Eco Warrior! Keep working to save the planet.

21 – 35
Not bad but you still have some work to do to be more green.

0 – 20
A lot of work to do. Remember, your actions affect the planet.
Why not make some changes today?

Activity 8 – Answer the Questions: Green Schools

The Green-Schools Programme has helped thousands of students and teachers to play a part in reducing Ireland's carbon footprint. Read the article below and answer the questions.

The Green-Schools Programme has been an enormous success in Ireland. There are over 3,400 schools registered on the programme; that represents 75% of all the schools in Ireland.

In this time of economic downturn, government departments are keeping a close eye on their spending. The Department of Education and Science will be happy to learn that the Green-Schools Programme is helping them to save money.

Recent research has revealed the Green-Schools Programme has huge economic value for Irish schools. The programme has saved schools a minimum €2 million in waste, electricity, water and fuel costs this year. The results reveal that a minimum of 12 tonnes of waste has been diverted from landfills in Ireland by schools undertaking the programme. 3.7 million units of electricity, 200 million litres of drinking water and around 500,000 litres of transport fuel were saved this year alone.

Because the programme also involves the wider community, the savings to the Irish economy are greater than the €2 million reported. Next year's savings are set to increase as the number of schools participating is growing year on year. Who says being green doesn't pay?

Information from www.greenschoolsireland.org

1 How many schools are involved in the Green-Schools Programme?
_____

2 According to the article, in what ways has the Green-Schools Programme benefited the environment?
_____
_____
_____
_____

3 Why will the Department of Education and Science be happy with the results of the Green-Schools Programme?
_____
_____
_____
_____

Activity 9 – Go Find Out: Current Ministers

Find out who the following ministers are. Insert a picture from the internet or the newspaper. *Hint:* go to www.gov.ie to get information.

Minister for the Environment, Heritage and Local Government
Name: _____

Minister for Communications, Energy and Natural Resources
Name: _____

Activity 10 – Go Find Out: Local Recycling Questionnaire

Research the recycling facilities in your local area and fill in the following questionnaire.

1 Do you have a green-bin service in your area for recyclable goods (plastic, etc.)?
Yes ❏   No ❏

2 Do you have a brown-bin service in your area (garden waste / compost)?
Yes ❏   No ❏

3 Do you have a local recycling centre?   Yes ❏   No ❏

If so, list the items that can be recycled there.

_____
_____
_____
_____

4 Name all the charity shops in your area that take items such as clothes and books to be re-used.

_____
_____
_____

5 Do you have a local service for recycling Christmas trees?   Yes ❏   No ❏

Activity 11 - Get Writing: Recycling

Having completed the questionnaire in Activity 10, rate your local authority out of ten for their commitment to recycling. Then write a letter either congratulating them or demanding an improvement in service. Write a draft of your letter below.

Your address here
→
_____
_____
_____
_____

Local authority
address here
↓

_____
_____
_____

Date here
→
_____

Dear
↘
_____

Write your letter here - be
polite and to the point!
↓

_____
_____
_____
_____
_____
_____
_____
_____
_____
_____
_____
_____
_____
_____
_____
_____
_____
_____

_____ ← 'Yours sincerely' if you know their
name; 'Yours faithfully' if you don't.

_____ ← Your name

Activity 12 – Get Writing: Conservation Organisations

The logos of four conservation organisations are shown. Name each organisation and write a description of what the organisation does.

1 _____
_____
_____
_____

2 _____
_____
_____
_____

3 _____
_____
_____
_____

4 _____
_____
_____
_____

WWF

GREENPEACE

SAVE THE RHINO
www.savetherhino.org

WDCS
Whale and Dolphin Conservation Society
www.adoptadolphin.org.au

Activity 13 – Exam Practice: Earth Summit

Study the cartoon and answer the questions below.

1.

2.

3.

4.

© Martyn Turner

1 To what global event is the cartoon referring?

_____ (2 marks)

2 Where did this event take place, and in what year?

Place: _____ **Year:** _____

(2 marks)

3 Why does the man in the cartoon believe it will take the environment years to recover from this global event?

_____
_____
_____ (2 marks)

4 What particular message do you think the person who drew this cartoon, Martyn Turner, is trying to give us?

_____
_____
_____ (4 marks)

5 Incinerators for burning waste have been suggested as one possible way of getting rid of the rubbish that we produce in Ireland. Give **ONE** reason why people might oppose the building of an incinerator, **AND ONE** reason why they might support the building of an incinerator.

Oppose: _____ **Support:** _____

_____ _____

(4 marks)

Adapted from Junior Certificate Exam

Activity 1 – Get Writing!

Explain each of the following:

Democracy

_____

_____

_____

Dictatorship

_____

_____

_____

Socialism

_____

_____

_____

Monarchy

_____

_____

_____

Anarchy

_____

_____

_____

Activity 2 – Word Search

Find the following words in the word search:
CONSTITUENCY – DÁIL – DEMOCRACY – ELECTION – GOVERNMENT – OIREACHTAS – REFERENDUM – SEANAD – TÁNAISTE – TAOISEACH – VOTE

```
T  Y  C  N  E  U  T  I  T  S  N  O  C  M  E
L  N  C  T  U  H  Y  U  F  Z  M  O  A  U  L
L  R  E  P  A  N  J  R  I  L  D  E  R  D  E
K  W  J  M  L  O  Q  C  G  I  S  E  T  N  C
I  Q  B  T  N  Y  I  Z  W  A  C  A  V  E  T
T  H  T  L  P  R  B  S  T  D  N  U  M  R  I
D  A  N  A  E  S  E  H  E  A  B  Z  B  E  O
Q  Z  G  K  I  X  C  V  I  A  T  L  V  F  N
E  W  W  K  M  A  M  S  O  I  C  G  M  E  E
O  T  C  N  E  O  T  B  V  G  Y  H  M  R  Z
C  B  O  R  U  E  K  G  T  R  E  W  G  G  P
M  F  I  V  G  A  E  A  D  E  Y  Y  U  S  O
R  O  E  C  H  F  S  J  A  Q  O  N  W  R  I
W  U  W  T  U  A  R  D  J  B  G  P  W  M  U
D  E  M  O  C  R  A  C  Y  Z  U  O  C  O  U
```

Activity 3 – Answer the Questions: Diary of a Suffragette

The suffragettes were a group of women who fought for democracy as they believed women should be allowed to vote alongside men. In this diary, a suffragette describes the part she played in the struggle for democracy. This is a powerful testimony to the endurance of these brave women.

12 May 1910, Holloway Prison

It's hard to believe that today is my birthday. I'd almost forgotten, so focused have I been on the struggle. Well this is one birthday I'll never forget. To be thrown in here like a common criminal is a disgrace, an indictment of our prejudicial society. When will we be given the status of political prisoners? When will the government realise that we are worthy of equal respect?

It is strange how public opinion is so divided. The policeman who arrested me confessed in a low voice that he too was a suffragette and wore our badge inside his helmet. He looked a little embarrassed telling me this and I can see why. When I was being led away from the demonstration a man passing me on the street sarcastically shouted, 'Votes for women, votes for donkeys, votes for dogs!' I won't let that kind of thing get me down though. I need to keep focused. I know that I have the support of the other suffragettes with me.

All the suffragettes knew what to do once we were arrested. When we all arrived in the prison, we stood together with our arms linked. I didn't know the suffragette beside me but immediately I felt connected to her. As a group we refused to go to our cells and demanded to see the governor. This was not granted and we were immediately placed in solitary confinement.

The doctor soon arrived but I refused to be medically examined or to wear prison clothes. Two wardresses then came in and roughly undressed me themselves. Although I didn't kick or scratch, I made it difficult for them to get the ghastly outfit on me. Once they left, I quickly took it off and retired to

bed. I know that every suffragette in this prison has done the same thing. We will not be treated as common criminals; our cause is political and we demand political status!

15 May 1910

It has been three days since I informed the wardress that I was on hunger strike. Although I am dreadfully hungry we must make it clear how serious our cause is. At first they placed a cup of steaming hot cocoa in my cell. It smelled so delicious and sweet but I tipped it on the floor to avoid temptation. A doctor was summoned to convince me to eat. He said, 'Young lady, if you continue to refuse to eat, I will have no choice but to have you forcibly fed; it is out of my hands.' To which I replied, 'It must be awful having choice taken away from you doctor.' I don't think he appreciated the irony.

True to his word, the doctor attempted to force-feed me. Two wardresses held me down while the doctor inserted a metal tube down my throat. I am sad to say that despite the amount of food that ended up on the floor, much of it was pumped into my stomach. It was truly a foul smelling liquid. I think the concoction was made up largely of cabbage and eggs.

All I can do is to continue to refuse food and clamp my mouth shut even tighter tomorrow. They may succeed in force-feeding me but I know if there are enough of us showing such determination, our message cannot fall on deaf ears for much longer.

Based on accounts given by Katherine Roberts, Constance Lytton and Emmeline Pankhurst

Activity 3 - Answer the Questions: Diary of a Suffragette

1   What right were the suffragettes campaigning for?
_____
_____

2   Why did the writer refuse to wear prison clothes?
_____
_____

3   Why were these women known as 'suffragettes'?
_____
_____

4   In Ireland Hannah Sheehy-Skeffington was a well-known suffragette campaigner. Using the internet or library sources, write a summary of her struggle for democracy.
_____
_____
_____
_____
_____
_____
_____
_____
_____
_____
_____
_____
_____
_____
_____
_____
_____

Activity 4 - Go Find Out: Nelson Mandela

**Nelson Mandela fought for democracy for all South Africans.
Go online or go to your library and research his life and struggle.**

The following key words may help you:
*   Apartheid
*   ANC (African National Congress)
*   Robben Island
*   Nobel Peace Prize
*   F.W. de Klerk
*   South African President

Activity 5 - Picture Perfect: Young People and the Vote

Design a poster to encourage young people to vote.

Activity 6 – Fill in the Gaps: Electoral Process in Ireland

Look at the section about voting in Ireland in your textbook and fill in the gaps below.

The voting system which we have in Ireland is called **P**_____
R _____. To be able to vote, a person must be at least eighteen
years of age and listed on the **R** _____ of **E** _____ .
Before the date of the election or referendum each voter receives a
P_____ card in the post. On election day, voters cast their votes at a
P_____ **S**_____ normally located in a local primary
school. There, voters fill in their choices of candidates on a **B** _____
paper and place it in a **B** _____ **B** _____.

Activity 7 – Go Find Out: Current Ministers

**Find out who the following ministers are. Insert a picture from the internet
or the newspaper. Hint: go to www.gov.ie to get information.**

Tánaiste
Name: _____
_____

Minister for Finance
Name: _____
_____

Minister for Education and
Science
Name: _____
_____

Minister for Foreign Affairs
Name: _____
_____

Minister for Justice,
Equality and Law Reform
Name: _____
_____

Minister for Health and
Children
Name: _____
_____

Activity 8 - True or False: Elections and Referenda

Read the statements below and tick the correct box.

		True	False
1	A by-election is held to fill one seat in Dáil Éireann following the death or resignation of a TD.	❏	❏
2	To change the constitution the people must vote in a referendum.	❏	❏
3	A General Election must be held every seven years.	❏	❏
4	Ireland is represented by fifteen MEPs in the European Parliament.	❏	❏
5	European Elections are held every four years.	❏	❏
6	A person elected to a local authority is called a councillor.	❏	❏
7	The people of Ireland are represented by 166 TDs in Dáil Éireann.	❏	❏
8	A person must be aged at least thirty-five years of age to run for the office of President of Ireland.	❏	❏
9	The Irish President's term of office is seven years.	❏	❏
10	The President's official residence is Áras an Uachtaráin.	❏	❏

Activity 9 - Match 'Em Up: Political Buildings

The following photographs are of three important political buildings in Ireland. Match them up correctly with the names given and write the correct name in the spaces provided below each building.

Áras an Uachtaráin   Leinster House   Northern Ireland Assembly, Stormont Castle

Name: _____   **Name:** _____   **Name:** _____

_____   _____   _____

Activity 10 – Get Writing: Write to Your Representative

Write to a politician (European, national or local) drawing his/her attention to an issue that you feel is important to you/your school/your community/Ireland (e.g. vandalism, class sizes, lowering the voting age etc.) Go to www.gov.ie or www.europa.eu for politicians' addresses.

Your address here

$\longrightarrow$ _____

_____

_____

Politician's
address here

$\downarrow$

Date here

$\longrightarrow$ _____

_____

_____

Name of politician you are writing to

Write your letter here - be
polite and to the point!

$\downarrow$

Dear $\longrightarrow$ _____

$\downarrow$

_____

_____

_____

_____

_____

_____

_____

_____

_____

_____

_____

_____

_____

_____

_____

_____

_____ $\longleftarrow$ **Yours sincerely,**

_____ $\longleftarrow$ Your name

Activity 11 – Exam Practice: Answer the Questions

Read the article below and answer the questions that follow.

Voting age must be lowered to give youth a real voice
Michael McLaughlin

Young people should be central to all decisions which affect them, and their voices should be heard across the board as often as possible. But will young people be able for such responsibility? Surely they will make stupid and ill-informed decisions? The same arguments were of course put about giving women the vote and extending the voting age to eighteen.

I had the pleasure of recently accompanying a group of young people to Geneva under the auspices of the Children's Rights Alliance to meet the United Nations Committee on the Rights of the Child. While escorting such a group naturally involved a bit of effort and time, the only occasion when I had no work to do was when the young people were speaking directly to the committee about their lives – after all, who knew this story better than they did?

Involving young people in decisions should not just be limited to sensitive or controversial issues; the day-to-day issues are just as important. Education is an obvious area where student councils mark the start of establishing young people as partners with teachers and parents. Public transport, policing, housing, taxation – why draw the line? A real say in society and full inclusion in decision-making will only come about with the extension of the franchise (voting age) to sixteen.

Michael McLaughlin is Director of Central Services with Youth Work Ireland and a board member of the Children's Rights Alliance.

Adapted from The Irish Times

(a) What argument is made against young people voting at sixteen?

_____

_____

Why were some young Irish people visiting Geneva?

_____

_____

(2 marks)

(b) From the newspaper article, name the **TWO** organisations working with children and young people.

First Organisation _____

Second Organisation _____

According to Michael McLaughlin, what will need to happen if young people are to have a real say in Irish society?

_____

_____

(3 marks)

(c) Suggest **TWO** ways in which you think society would gain from lowering the voting age to sixteen?
First Way _____
Second Way _____
(2 marks)

(d) Apart from lowering the voting age to sixteen, describe **TWO** actions **IRISH POLITICIANS** can take to involve young people more in politics.
First Action _____
_____
Second Action _____
_____
(4 marks)

(e) Imagine you have just been appointed by the Children's Rights Alliance to run a campaign to have the voting age lowered to sixteen. Write a slogan which you would use to encourage people to get involved in this campaign.
Campaign Slogan _____
_____
_____
(3 marks)

Adapted from Junior Certificate Exam

Activity 12 - Go Find Out: Your Local TD

Go online or call into your local TD's office in person and fill out the following profile.

Name: _____

Political Party: _____

Constituency: _____

Current Position:
(e.g. opposition TD, minister, junior minister, back bencher)
_____

Job/profession before being elected: _____
_____

Email: _____

Telephone: _____

Address: _____
_____
_____
_____

CONCEPT 5 Development

Activity 1 – Get Writing!

Explain each of the following:

Development

_____
_____
_____

Emergency Aid

_____
_____
_____

Development Aid

_____
_____
_____

Non-Governmental Organisation (NGO)

_____
_____
_____

Planning Permission

_____
_____
_____

Activity 2 – Word Search

Find the following words in the word search:

AID – CONCERN – DEBT – DEVELOPMENT – DROUGHT – ENVIRONMENT – EQUALITY
FOOD CRISIS – MICROCREDIT – NGO – PLANNING – TRADE – TRÓCAIRE

X	G	Y	T	A	Y	T	K	P	U	Q	T	S	T	N
U	A	W	N	S	F	A	H	A	D	N	F	R	W	R
T	G	E	E	L	T	O	D	G	E	Y	O	Y	K	E
I	M	I	M	K	B	E	O	M	U	C	P	R	H	C
P	R	Z	P	G	L	W	N	D	A	O	Q	O	S	N
L	P	J	O	B	L	O	Y	I	C	T	R	V	N	O
A	Y	L	L	K	R	P	R	J	Z	R	S	D	G	C
N	I	G	E	I	X	E	G	N	B	F	I	O	O	G
N	N	D	V	Y	T	I	L	A	U	Q	E	S	E	G
I	J	N	E	M	I	C	R	O	C	R	E	D	I	T
N	E	E	D	N	B	W	D	E	B	T	A	E	J	S
G	C	Z	J	O	Q	G	F	I	M	R	O	A	U	V
M	H	D	S	M	R	E	F	P	T	B	C	E	J	W
P	J	A	O	Y	M	S	P	O	Q	J	L	X	E	J
X	I	M	V	T	N	G	Y	K	T	Y	P	F	Z	N

Activity 3 - Match 'Em Up: National or Local

Look at the list of developments A-J below and place them under the correct heading, depending on whether they are national or local developments.

A Extension to M12 Motorway planned
B New recycling facility opened
C Plans for socially affordable housing announced
D School sought for growing Muslim community
E Swimming pool upgraded to 50m pool
F New hospital to be built to cater for growing community
G Upgrading of railway line to the Northwest postponed due to economic crisis
H Extra gardaí recruited to deal with gun crime
I Farmers get permission for weekend market in park
J Community promised new Fire Brigade service after recent tragedy

Local Development

_____
_____
_____
_____
_____
_____
_____

National Development

_____
_____
_____
_____
_____
_____
_____

Activity 4 - Get Writing: Community Development

A piece of land has become available in your locality and you have joined a campaign to have this land used for a skateboarding park for young people and a community centre.

In the space below, write a letter to one of your local councillors, inviting him/her to attend a public meeting on the issue. In your letter refer to your campaign and outline three reasons why this development is needed.

Your address here →
_____
_____
_____
_____

Councillor's address here
↓

Date here →
_____

_____
_____
_____

Name of Councillor you are writing to
↓

Dear _____

Write your letter here - be polite and to the point!
↓

_____
_____
_____
_____
_____
_____
_____
_____
_____
_____
_____
_____
_____
_____
_____
_____

_____ ← **Yours sincerely,**

_____ ← Your name

Activity 5 – Answer the Questions: Controversial Developments

Living in the shadow of Ireland's first waste incinerator

Despite ten years of local opposition, construction work began on the highly controversial waste incinerator at Carranstown, Duleek – Ireland's first commercial incinerator. The €130 million incinerator has been bitterly opposed in a ten-year battle by the local community, who have held meetings, raised money, hired experts, and have even gone as far as the Supreme Court in their objections to the development.

The facility will process 200,000 tonnes of waste each year. The contract for the work was awarded to an international firm but is supported by an Irish construction company. During the building phase, an estimated 300 people have been employed, with a further sixty jobs available once the plant is operational.

The incinerator project was the most controversial planning application ever to come before Meath County Council with more than 4,000 individual objections to the original planning application and a petition signed by 27,000 people.

Objectors have claimed that the incinerator could have a devastating effect on local health, the environment and on local farms. They say that incineration produces toxins that are harmful to the health of communities.

Other residents have safety concerns regarding the extra traffic. One couple, whose home is a stone's throw from the site, said 'It seems to us that Duleek is just being used as a dumping ground. The traffic is going to be awful. It's already lethal with people flying through here commuting between Drogheda and Dublin. What's it going to be like with those trucks coming in and out?'

Duleek used to be a village. Now it is swamped by housing estates. Six miles down the road, the village of Laytown was in the news over a shortage of school places as the infrastructure failed to keep pace with frantic house-building.

Many in the No Incineration Alliance (NIA) feel that their village is being used as a dumping ground for the state's first incinerator. 'It's a health issue, pure and simple,' said one local woman. However, the health issue is nearly impossible to determine. The World Health Organisation has given the green light to incinerators if properly monitored, but serious questions still remain about the amount and dangers of pollutants emitted through the process.

'I have three children, it's them I'm worried about,' said one mother, 'Children breathe much quicker, they take in pollutants. And anyway, nobody can guarantee there won't be an accident at that site. What then?'

Adapted from an article in *The Meath Chronicle*

1 Why is the incinerator in Duleek a controversial development?

_____

_____

_____

2 List **ONE** benefit of this development to the local community, according to the article.

_____

_____

_____

3 List **TWO** concerns that the local community have.

(a) _____

_____

(b) _____

_____

4 How has poor planning added to problems in the area?

_____

_____

_____

_____

5 Can you suggest **ONE** alternative way of dealing with waste that would reduce the need for incineration? Explain your answer.

_____

_____

_____

_____

Activity 6 – Picture Perfect: Tidy Towns

Your class is hoping to help develop your local area by getting involved in the Tidy Towns Competition. Design a poster to encourage your local community to take part in a Clean Up and Planting Day in your town. Don't forget to add a slogan.

Activity 7 – Answer the Questions: Local Authority

Read the passage below and answer the questions that follow:

Brian O'Driscoll: The new face of credit unions

'Credit unions are based in the heart of local communities and have a real understanding of the needs of their members. Credit unions are all about people. They exist to serve members, not to profit from their needs.' These are the words of Kieron Brennan, Chief Executive of the Irish League of Credit Unions, when celebrating International Credit Union Day on 15 October.

Credit unions are voluntary financial cooperatives which provide financial services to their members. They differ from banks in that they are owned by their members, not shareholders, and do not seek to profit from the needs of their members.

Credit unions are truly at the economic heart of a community. In Ireland there are 530 credit unions with 2.9 million members and €13.4 billion in assets. This mirrors the importance of credit unions internationally where 177 million credit union members control €870 billion in assets.

Credit unions provide community-based lending. They use the savings from their members to lend to those who need such things as home improvements, education, a car or a holiday. In this way one member of the community is helping another in the true spirit of 'community'. Many small savers, people on low incomes or those experiencing financial difficulties, who may not qualify for a bank loan, can turn to their credit union where they may be personally known, and where all their circumstances are taken into consideration. In this way credit unions seek to serve the community.

Earlier this year, international rugby player Brian O'Driscoll became the new face of Irish credit unions. O'Driscoll commented, 'I am delighted to have become involved with the credit union movement at this time. I believe it is an important time for our communities and I have always greatly admired the valuable role that credit unions have played in fostering a sense of belonging and team work.'

1 Who is the new face of Irish credit unions, and why does he believe credit unions are an important part of a community?

_____
_____
_____
_____

2 Mention **ONE** difference between banks and credit unions.

_____
_____
_____

3 How do credit unions display true 'community spirit' according to this article?

_____
_____
_____

4 Go find out where your local credit union is. Write the address below and how you or your family could benefit from being members.

_____
_____
_____
_____
_____

Activity 8 - True or False

Read the statements below and tick the appropriate box.

		True	False
1	All major developments in Ireland require planning permission.	❏	❏
2	An Bord Pleanála has the final say in planning appeals.	❏	❏
3	The Tidy Towns competition is run by the Department of the Environment, Heritage and Local Government.	❏	❏
4	Nearly everybody in the world has access to safe drinking water.	❏	❏
5	The Millennium Development Goals aim to halve hunger by next year.	❏	❏
6	Biofuels are helping to end the international Food Crisis.	❏	❏
7	80% of people live in the Developing World.	❏	❏
8	John O'Shea founded the charity, Bóthar.	❏	❏
9	Nearly 1 billion people across the globe are illiterate.	❏	❏
10	Every 3.6 seconds somebody dies from hunger.	❏	❏

Read the case study and answer the questions that follow:

Activity 9 – Match 'Em Up: Development Organisations

Look at the organisations below and draw arrows to match them to the correct description.

This NGO aims to help those in the developing world by providing livestock and animals so that they can start their own farms.

This organisation was founded in 1977 by John O'Shea. It has provided development and emergency aid to over 50 countries.

This organisation is funded by the Irish Government and is involved with providing development aid around the world.

This group is funded by the Catholic Church and aims to tackle poverty, climate change and inequality through long-term development aid.

This NGO works with local people to help tackle a number of problems. One of its schemes includes providing aid through a mobile phone money transfer scheme.

Activity 10 – Answer the Questions: Microcredit

Collecting for the Future – Microfinance in Bangladesh

The urban slum areas of Saidpur in Northern Bangladesh are home to some of Bangladesh's poorest people. Most people live in overcrowded shacks with no clean water or electricity. Increasingly, these areas are home to 'floating populations' of homeless people who sleep on the streets at night. Imran was one such person. An elderly man with no family, no way of earning a living and very few possessions, Imran had been homeless for most of his life. He felt ashamed to be a burden on his community. Although trapped in a cycle of poverty, Imran had an idea of how he could get himself out. He just needed the means to do so.

Imran's idea was to support himself through the sale of firewood. Most of the people in the urban slum community in which he lived needed wood for cooking and to boil water for washing and drinking. However, they had to walk for some distance to get this firewood which took up valuable time. This meant that adults lost work-time and children often missed school.

Imran felt that if he could collect the firewood and sell it to families at a reasonable price, he would not only be supporting himself, but providing a service to the community at the same time. To do this, he needed credit to rent a stall and to buy the necessary equipment. In the past he would not have been able to get credit as he had nothing to use as collateral, which would guarantee that he would be able to pay back a loan. The interest rates of the moneylenders would have been too high and too much of a risk.

One day, Imran heard of a group savings scheme in the community, supported by Concern, where he could take out a loan even though he had no assets. By collecting and selling wood and using his stall as his new accommodation, Imran soon paid off his loan and was able to start saving for his future. Not only is he now self-sufficient, but through his savings he is helping other members of the group to access credit and get out of poverty. Imran is just one of more than 45,000 people supported by Concern's microfinance programme in Bangladesh.

1 Why couldn't Imran get credit in the past?
   _____
   _____

2 Describe Imran's business idea and why it was of benefit to other members of the community.
   _____
   _____
   _____
   _____

3 How did Concern's microcredit programme improve Imran's life?
   _____
   _____
   _____
   _____

4 How does microcredit help poor communities develop?
   _____
   _____
   _____

Activity 11 – Exam Practice: Development Aid

When Niall Mellon saw first-hand the poverty in the townships in South Africa, he set up the Niall Mellon Township Trust in 2002 to provide homes to the poor communities in the townships. Volunteers from Ireland raise money and travel to South Africa to build houses in the townships.

From This . . .

To This . . .

Living in a shack has been shown to have a negative impact on health, education and self-esteem.

***

Without a sense of home, people's self-respect can be diminished.

***

Without basic housing, families are not equipped to face the other challenges poverty brings like crime, poor education, inadequate nutrition, decaying neighbourhoods and sub-standard healthcare.

Most of the workforce comes from the townships themselves. Community development is a central part of the work of the Niall Mellon Township Trust working with local communities in the planning and design of the new communities.

in partnership with

Irish Aid

Department of Foreign Affairs
An Roinn Gnóthaí Eachtracha

Adapted from www.irishtownship.com

1 What inspired Niall Mellon to set up this trust?

_____

_____

In what year was the Niall Mellon Township Trust set up?

_____

What does the Niall Mellon Township Trust do?

_____

_____

(3 marks)

2 From your reading of the information leaflet, name **THREE** challenges that poverty brings.

First challenge _____

Second challenge _____

Third challenge _____

(3 marks)

3 Why do you think it is important for local communities to get involved in projects like the Niall Mellon Township Trust?

_____

_____

(2 marks)

4 A teacher from your school has volunteered to travel to South Africa to build houses with the Niall Mellon Township Trust. Name and describe **ONE** fundraising activity **YOUR SCHOOL** could undertake to help this teacher.

Name of activity _____

Description _____

_____

(2 marks)

5 Name and describe **TWO** other actions **YOUR COMMUNITY** could take that would help to make it possible for this teacher to go to South Africa.

First action _____

Description _____

_____

Second action_____

Description _____

_____

(4 marks)

Adapted from Junior Certificate Exam

Activity 12 – Answer the Questions: Development in Action

In the passage below we find out how Eimear Broderick and Emma McGuire, two fifth-year students from The Teresian Secondary School, played a part in developing a small Peruvian community.

In a remote village outside Via El Salvador in Peru, life used to be very difficult. The community of ten houses and one school had never had access to electricity. This meant that children could only go to school for a few hours a day as they had to work in the morning and there was not enough light for them to study in the evening. Life at home was also a challenge. Without electricity, cooking and heating were constant problems. The people were so poor that the children went to the Wa-Wa-Wasis, charitable crèches where they could be fed.

The Teresian School already had a strong link with the Latin world as the school was founded by a Spanish religious order. Eimear, Emma and their classmates decided they could make a difference to these people's lives. The girls raised €1,500 through bag-packing, event days and corporate sponsorship. This was enough to buy solar panels for the small community.

The class and their teacher, Anne Marie Alverez, went to Peru and helped install the solar panels with the community. There were huge celebrations when the first lightbulb came on. The girls knew that they had changed the lives of these people forever.

Now, the village's children have electricity in their school. This will give them a chance of escaping the poverty trap. In their homes, lights keep out the gloom in the evenings and electric ovens warm the kitchens.

1 Other than 'Development', what CSPE concepts does the girls' project relate to?

_____

_____

_____

2 How did the girls raise the funds for the solar panels?

_____

_____

_____

3 How did the solar panels change the lives of the people?

_____

_____

_____

_____

4 How will this action help in the long term development of the community?

_____

_____

_____

_____

Activity 1 - Get Writing!

Explain each of the following:

Law _____
_____

Criminal Law _____
_____

Civil Law _____
_____

Bye-Laws _____
_____

Bill _____
_____

Activity 2 - Word Search

Find the following words in the word search:
ACT – BARRISTER – BILL – CIVIL – COURT – CRIMINAL – GARDA – JURY – LAW
OMBUDSMAN – PRISON – PROBATION – SOLICITOR

V	C	R	E	V	K	C	H	C	V	L	E	R	V	C
B	G	Z	M	T	R	I	F	J	M	A	N	S	X	E
G	A	R	D	A	B	V	O	I	E	N	H	N	Y	D
G	C	U	E	V	T	I	Z	E	F	I	N	E	P	B
I	O	F	D	X	L	L	C	D	E	M	F	G	I	R
T	Y	V	O	O	R	R	P	V	G	I	C	L	T	F
W	O	E	D	K	L	O	K	V	P	R	L	P	I	Q
R	M	O	I	G	H	Q	T	R	K	C	E	I	N	H
L	B	P	X	M	I	P	O	I	F	X	H	O	G	Q
T	U	U	O	W	T	B	O	A	C	N	S	A	H	K
C	D	C	U	H	A	R	E	T	S	I	R	R	A	B
A	S	Q	O	T	Y	R	U	J	R	W	L	S	V	I
J	M	F	I	U	O	S	U	P	M	L	A	O	H	S
U	A	O	E	D	R	A	N	I	E	B	J	L	S	E
M	N	O	Y	Q	A	T	S	L	M	M	M	V	Q	M

Activity 3 - Get Writing: Why do we need Laws?

Read the following scenario and complete the exercise.

On your return from a school trip, an outbreak of swine flu has been confirmed among the students. All the staff have been evacuated and the students are being held in isolation. Draw up a list of the **FIVE** rules which you think are most important to ensure safety and fairness for everyone until the quarantine ends.

The Five Rules

_____

_____

_____

_____

_____

_____

Activity 4 - Fill in the Gaps: Enforcing the Law

The Law in Ireland is enforced by An Garda **S**_____, the Army and through the court system. This discourages people from breaking the law.

The Gardaí are the police force in Ireland. They are managed by the Garda **C**_____ who reports to the Minister for **J**_____, Equality and Law Reform. The Gardaí are one of the few police forces in the world who don't carry guns; instead they have a **B**_____. The Garda training centre is in **T**_____ in Co. Tipperary. To ensure that they do not abuse their powers, complaints about gardaí can be made to the Garda **O**_____.

The Irish court system is divided up into two groups: Criminal Courts and **C**_____ Courts. Almost all criminal cases begin in the **D**_____ Court.

If an individual is unhappy with the decision this court has made, they have the right to appeal to the **C**_____ Court. The highest court is the **S**_____ Court. Decisions made here are written into law and are known as Common Law or **C**_____ Law.

There are many people in a court room who help a case to proceed. At the top of the court sits the **J**_____. He / she runs the trial or hearing and ensures that it is fair and just. He / she is assisted by the **T**_____ who announces when the judge is arriving or leaving by calling 'All Rise'. During trials, cases are made by **B**_____, who are legal experts trained to speak in court.

During criminal trials a **J**_____ decides if an individual is guilty or not. This is a group of twelve people. Their decision, known as a **V**_____, is read out by the group's foreman.

An Garda Síochána
Crime Prevention Information Sheet

PROPERTY CRIME
GRAFFITI

Graffiti - a costly menace!

Uncontrolled graffiti is criminal damage and against the law. To the perpetrator it may be intended as a form of artistic expression, a threatening or abusive message or just a wanton act of destructive vandalism. Unfortunately, like all other acts of criminal damage, there are economic costs for the injured parties and many other undesirable results for society in general.

Undesired and permanent graffiti sends out the strong social message that the property is not respected, is not under proper control and the area is not an attractive place to live or work. If graffiti is not removed it can also encourage other acts of vandalism and eventually lead to the growth of hostile and uncontrolled environments. It can start a cycle of decay which, if not tackled or controlled, also generates greater fear and alienation for people who must live and work in these areas.

It is important to realise that graffiti is not the work of an 'unknown or aspiring artist' but an act of criminal damage that encourages further criminal acts and has economic and social costs that must be borne by everybody.

Graffiti also means:

- Clean-up costs that can vary greatly depending on the surface being defaced
- Unsightly defacement of structures
- Increased fear of crime
- Encouragement of other forms of crime and vandalism
- Reduced attraction or incentive to live and work in the area
- Falling property prices
- Reduced inward investment and employment

Does graffiti have a pattern?

Most graffiti is committed by people who are generally within three groups or categories.
Firstly, there are 'writers'. These are usually responsible for some of the more flamboyant or artistic styles of graffiti. They will usually work in small groups and display their work in highly visible locations such as the tops of buildings, on bridge structures or underpasses. They will take great time and effort, including risks, to display their work. This can then lead to further competition from similarly minded individuals and a proliferation of the problem. Secondly, there are 'taggers' who are generally individuals who have a personalised or stylised signature or writing. Their motivation is usually to deface as many areas as possible with their own work. Finally, there may be an identified gang or unlawful groups who want to send a message. This message, generally intended to be threatening, is usually written in a highly visible location.

By and large, however, graffiti vandals are usually teenagers or young persons. If you are a parent or guardian you should watch for tell-tale signs that your children are involved in this activity, such as the possession of spray paint cans and markers or paint residue on their fingers and clothes. They may also have heavily marked personal property or books - could you as a parent identify your child's 'tag'?

FOR FURTHER INFORMATION ON THIS OR OTHER CRIME PREVENTION ISSUES,
PLEASE CONTACT your local GARDA CRIME PREVENTION OFFICER
or
visit the Garda website at www.garda.ie

Graffiti Prevention and Control

The best way of preventing graffiti is to consider the potential areas where it may occur during the planning and design stages of buildings. This will involve carefully choosing the surfaces of the wall or building and limiting the areas available to write on. A textured wall and minimal large bare surfaces will be less attractive to the graffiti vandal. Generally, the more porous the surface the more difficult it will be to clean. Wood and brick will be more attractive than metal structures or oil-based painted areas.

In established areas the spread of graffiti can be prevented with the strategic use of plants, such as thorny hedging or fast growing creepers, on vulnerable walls. The use of large blank walls or areas for legitimate advertising or display should be considered. In indoor areas, particularly public toilets, the use of designated graffiti boards can greatly limit the damage to walls and doors out of public view.

The best form of graffiti control is swift and proper clean up. This will stop a copycat style spread and limit its recurrence. It also demonstrates that there is ownership and control of the property and frustrates the work of the vandal. Graffiti operators are unlikely to return to areas where they have invested their time and money, to find that their work is always removed immediately. The entire surface area that has been defaced should be cleaned or repainted and not just spot covering the affected area as this can encourage repeat offences by the culprit.

Defaced window and doors

Defaced parking meter

Defaced recycling bins and utility cabinet

Defaced pavement and traffic sign

Spot covering - not recommended

It is very important that persons employed in graffiti removal are made aware of black spots and use materials or paints that will dissuade a potential recurrence.

The following photographs give an idea of how graffiti can deface a neighbourhood and common-place items therein. There is nothing attractive in this type of behaviour – it shows a complete disregard and contempt for people living in the area, their property and the environment as a whole.

The advice contained in this information sheet is not intended to be exhaustive or absolute.

Nothing contained in this publication should be interpreted as mandatory, obligatory or designed to conflict with any statutory regulations.

Useful Contacts and Links
The Garda National Crime
Prevention Unit,
Garda H.Q., Harcourt Square, Dublin 2.
Tel: (01) 6663362 Fax: (01) 6663314
Email: crime_prevention@garda.ie
An Garda Síochána
www.garda.ie

Activity 5 – Answer the Questions: Graffiti

Read the leaflet from the Garda Crime Prevention Unit on the previous pages and answer the following questions.

1   List **THREE** negative consequences of graffiti from the leaflet.

   (a) _____

   _____

   (b) _____

   _____

   (c) _____

   _____

2   According to the leaflet, who are the groups of people who take part in graffiti?

   (a) _____

   (b) _____

   (c) _____

3   On the second page, advice is given about how to prevent graffiti. Write down **TWO** of these tips below.

   (a) _____

   _____

   (b) _____

   _____

4   The leaflet claims that 'graffiti vandals are usually teenagers or young persons.' Is this a fair statement to make? Explain your answer.

   _____

   _____

   _____

   _____

5   Do you think this leaflet is an effective method of preventing graffiti? Can you think of another way of tackling this problem? Explain your answer.

   _____

   _____

   _____

   _____

   _____

Activity 6 – Picture Perfect: Neighbourhood Watch

Your local Community Garda is keen to start a neighbourhood watch programme. Design a flyer to encourage the local residents to take part. Include important information, lots of colour and a slogan.

Activity 7 – Match 'Em Up: Who's Who in the Court?

Look at the courtroom scene below and match the names to the correct spaces.

Tipstaff

Jury

Solicitors

Stenographer

Judge

Barrister

Prison Officer

The press

Registrar

Witness

The public

Accused

Activity 8 – Fill in the Gaps: Who Does What in the Courtroom?

Fill in the speech bubbles below to describe the duties of the various people in court.

I am a judge. My job is to
_____
_____
_____
_____
_____

I am a solicitor, I make sure
that _____
_____
_____
_____

Barristers like me are
employed to _____
_____
_____
_____

The job of the
stenographer is to _____
_____
_____
_____
_____

Members of the media
often attend court cases
to _____
_____
_____
_____

I am the Registrar of the
court. My job is _____
_____
_____
_____
_____

Activity 9 – Match 'Em Up: The Courts

COURTS

District Court

Court of Criminal Appeal

Supreme Court

Special Criminal Court

High Court

Children's Court

Write the names of the courts beside the correct descriptions.

1 This is the highest court in Ireland. It deals with appeals from the High Court and cases about the constitution.
Name of Court _____

2 This court has no jury and deals with serious crimes such as terrorism.
Name of Court _____

3 This court deals with offences committed by young people under the age of sixteen.
Name of Court _____

4 This is the second-highest court in the Irish legal system. It hears appeals from lower courts.
Name of Court _____

5 When a person convicted of a crime does not agree with the judgement given in the Central Criminal Court they may appeal to this court.
Name of Court _____

6 This court hears both criminal and civil cases. There are twenty-three courts like this around the country.
Name of Court _____

Activity 10 – Quiz: Consumer Rights

Answer the following questions to see how well you know your consumer rights. Write the letter of your chosen answer in the box.

1 You recently bought an MP3 player but it's faulty so you return to the shop with it. The shop insists on a receipt but you don't have one as your mum threw it out in the recycling bin. Do you…
(a) Leave the shop feeling foolish with the faulty MP3 player as you always have to have a receipt for a refund?
(b) Show the shop the credit card statement as proof of purchase?
(c) Sue your mum?

2 Your brand-new T-shirt shrinks in the washing machine. The care instructions say 'Hand-wash only'. Are you entitled to…
(a) A full refund from the shop?
(b) Nothing, but you could tell your friends that tight T-shirts are all the rage?
(c) A replacement T-shirt from the manufacturer?

3 Your new laptop which your mum bought you on an Irish website turns out to be faulty. What should she do?
(a) Decide never to buy anything online again?
(b) Ask for a refund, repair or replacement?
(c) Call the Garda Bureau of Fraud Investigation immediately?

4   You take your 'great bargain' X-Box out of the packaging when you get home
     from the sales but it doesn't work. You bring it back to the shop but the sales assistant
     points to signs saying 'Strictly no refunds'. Do you…
     (a) Go away empty-handed?
     (b) Demand a refund anyway – and complain to the National Consumer Agency?
     (c) Call the Gardaí?

5   You put some food in your shopping trolley, but at the checkout they say it's much
     dearer than the price on the shelf label. Do you…
     (a) Pay the higher price because you have to, now that you're at the till?
     (b) Warn the shop they may be breaking the law?
     (c) Insist on the lower price?

6   You buy a jumper but a day later you notice the sleeve is torn. When you bring it back,
     the shop has no more jumpers in your size. They offer you a refund, but only at a lower
     price because the sales are on. Do you…
     (a) Accept the lower price?
     (b) Refuse to take the lower amount, as the jumper is not fit for its intended
              purpose?
     (c) Sue the shop for emotional distress?

7   You arrive at check-in on time for your flight but the airline says it's overbooked and
     they can't give you an alternative flight that day. Should you…
     (a) Do nothing. Why bother, it's a low-cost flight?
     (b) Complain there and then, as you know you are entitled to a refund and
              compensation of €250 for being denied boarding?
     (c) Cause a scene and demand free flights for life?

8   You order a DVD of a foreign film from a website in France. When it arrives you realise
     it doesn't have English subtitles (although the website did actually say this). Do you…
     (a) Arrange for French grinds so that you can understand it?
     (b) Cancel your order immediately?
     (c) Keep it – it might come in handy if you ever have a French boyfriend/girlfriend?

9   Your friend gave you a gift voucher from your favourite shop for your birthday, but you
     lost it on the way home from the party. Do you…
     (a) Go to the shop anyway and ask for a refund?
     (b) Feel sorry for yourself but accept there's nothing you can do?
     (c) Confess to your friend and hope she'll buy you another one?

10   You are filling in your order on a website to buy some CDs. The web address begins
     'https://' and there's a padlock symbol in the bottom right corner of the screen. Do you…
     (a) Log off immediately as this means the page is not safe?
     (b) Proceed – the page is secure?
     (c) Sit there and wait – this symbol means the page is 'locked'?

If you scored mostly **'a's** – sorry but you're definitely not a clever consumer and you need
to read up on your rights. Log onto www.consumerconnect.ie
If you scored mostly **'b's** – well done! You seem to really know your consumer rights.
If you scored mostly **'c's** – you really are an optimist.

Activity 11 – Crossword

Across

6. The Garda _____ is the head of An Garda Síochána (12)
8. The type of sentence given to a person when they are sent to prison (9)
9. The person who handles complaints made about Gardaí (9)
11. The International Court of Justice is held in this Dutch city (5)

Down

1. The Director of Public _____ decides whether to bring criminal cases to trial (12)
2. The highest court in the land (7)
3. This convention was made in Switzerland to limit the effects of war on individuals (7)
4. A group of twelve people who decide whether a person is guilty or not (4)
5. A judge's personal assistant who announces 'All Rise' (8)
7. The person who records what was said in court (12)
10. A proposed new law (4)

Activity 12 - Exam Practice: The Courts

The Four Courts

The courts play a very important role in our society, but many people have never visited a court building. Your **CSPE** class has decided to organise a visit to The Four Courts in Dublin to help you understand the role that the courts play.

1   Name and explain **TWO** activities you could undertake before your visit in order to help you understand how the courts work.

_____
_____
_____
_____

(6 marks)

2   Write a letter to The Courts Service Information Office asking for a guided tour of The Four Courts for your **CSPE** class. In your letter you should mention **TWO** reasons why you and your classmates would like to visit the court.

_____
_____
_____
_____
_____
_____
_____
_____
_____
_____

(6 marks)

3   Apart from letter writing, describe in detail the work of **THREE** groups that you would set up in order to organise your class visit to The Four Courts.

_____
_____
_____
_____
_____
_____
_____
_____
_____

(8 marks)

Adapted from Junior Certificate Exam

CONCEPT 7 Interdependence

Activity 1 - Get Writing!

Explain each of the following.

Interdependence

_____

_____

_____

Globalisation

_____

_____

_____

Fairtrade

_____

_____

_____

Transnational Corporations

_____

_____

_____

_____

Activity 2 - Word Search

Find the following words in the word search:
COMMISSION – EURO – EUROPE – FAIRTRADE – GLOBALISATION –
INTERDEPENDENCE – MEP – TRADE – TREATY – UNITED NATIONS

T	B	Z	S	Z	I	F	A	I	R	T	R	A	D	E
R	U	E	N	E	N	S	P	A	I	M	D	J	R	Q
E	D	N	O	I	T	A	S	I	L	A	B	O	L	G
A	Y	N	I	S	E	E	P	J	G	W	Z	Y	Q	K
T	S	C	T	K	R	Q	U	E	P	U	L	L	K	N
Y	V	A	A	S	D	U	J	R	M	S	H	M	O	F
Q	G	R	N	X	E	D	G	P	O	T	R	I	J	G
P	T	K	D	Q	P	A	Y	O	R	P	S	E	V	P
O	R	U	E	S	E	P	B	A	M	S	E	H	I	X
H	D	I	T	R	N	B	D	V	I	J	G	E	F	O
V	F	D	I	Y	D	E	Q	M	N	M	K	D	Q	K
Z	N	E	N	W	E	J	M	F	Y	M	K	V	B	I
G	H	W	U	L	N	O	L	G	N	F	L	S	B	C
H	W	Y	V	N	C	I	I	K	L	M	F	Y	P	C
H	C	J	I	I	E	I	B	Q	U	A	X	K	Q	C

Activity 3 - Survey: Interdependence

See how many connections you have to the wider world. Fill in the survey below and see if you know someone who:

1 **. . . has a relative living in another country**

Name of person _____ Country _____

2 **. . . has purchased something from another country online recently**

Name of person _____ Product and country_____

_____

3 **. . . can speak a foreign language**

Name of person _____ Language_____

4 **. . . heard something about another country on TV recently**

Name of person _____ Country _____

5 **. . . has emailed a friend in another country**

Name of person _____ Country _____

6 **. . . has travelled to another country on business or holiday**

Name of person _____ Country _____

7 **. . . is wearing something made in another country**

Name of person _____ Country _____

Activity 4 – Answer the Questions: Sweatshops and Fairtrade

Give Bad Balls the Boot

It's a little known fact that around three-quarters of the world's footballs are made in Sialkot in Pakistan. It takes 700 hand-stitches to make a football. An experienced stitcher can make up to five balls a day. The work is tiring and often done in poor conditions. Men, women and children work long hours for little pay. As children have to work, there is often no time for school.

In 1997 UNICEF placed pressure on sports brands to improve working conditions for children. Nike, Adidas, Puma and Reebok all signed an agreement that they would not employ stitchers under the age of fourteen. The next year FIFA banned the use of footballs made using child labour. This was a step in the right direction; by 2002, three manufacturers had begun to make Fairtrade certified footballs that were soon available to consumers around the world.

Workers in these companies have experienced a huge improvement in their quality of life. Pay has risen, allowing children to go to school, and families can now have their basic needs met. Working conditions also improved dramatically. Fairtrade factories have a decent standard of light, ventilation and safe drinking water. Workers receive information on their wages and rights in their native language, Urdu.

The Fairtrade Social Premium is about 20% of the cost price of the balls. This money goes towards health clinics, business credit schemes, irrigation projects and education. Nursery care is also provided so that women can leave their children somewhere safe while they work.

Fairtrade has made a big difference to many families, but it only accounts for a small fraction of the balls produced in Sialkot. So why not make sure your sports equipment is Fairtrade certified and help level the playing field?

Adapted from *50 Reasons to Buy Fairtrade* by Miles Litvinoff and John Madeley,

1 What was the 'step in the right direction' that eventually led to Fairtrade football manufacturers in Sialkot being set up?

_____

_____

_____

2 What changes did Fairtrade bring to the workers' lives?

_____

_____

_____

3 What was the Fairtrade Social Premium spent on?

_____

_____

_____

4 What does the article suggest that you should do?

_____

_____

_____

Activity 5 – Answer the Questions: Benefits of Fairtrade

Study the article and answer the questions that follow:

Kit Kat gives cocoa farmers in Côte d'Ivoire a break

Fairtrade Mark Ireland today welcomed the announcement that Kit Kat, Ireland's best-selling chocolate biscuit bar, is going Fairtrade! This development follows the launch of Cadbury Fairtrade Dairy Milk bars, which became the first ever mass-market Fairtrade chocolate.

The Kit Kat move is set to benefit thousands of farmers in Côte d'Ivoire (Ivory Coast) in Africa, which is one of the world's poorest countries. According to the World Bank, nearly 50% of people in Côte d'Ivoire live below the poverty line. At least 4,300 tonnes of cocoa for Kit Kat will come from Côte d'Ivoire, and farmers there are now guaranteed not only a fair price but a Fairtrade premium of US$150 per tonne.

Fulgence Nguessan, President of Kavokiva Co-operative in the African country, was delighted with the news saying that the move will help to improve the living conditions of its 6,000 farmer-members. He added that a significant part of the Fairtrade premium would be used to ensure that all children can attend school as well as providing better healthcare services for the community.

Irish consumers rank among the biggest consumers of chocolate in the world, and are already highly committed to Fairtrade. Now they can give an even bigger break to cocoa farmers as they enjoy their favourite bar!

1 Name **TWO** new Fairtrade chocolate bars available in Ireland.

_____

_____

2 List **TWO** ways in which the Fairtrade Kit Kat bar will benefit the farmers in Côte d'Ivoire.

(a) _____

(b) _____

3 How much extra is paid to the farmers as a Fairtrade premium, and how does it help to improve the living conditions of the cocoa farmers?

_____

_____

_____

4 List **THREE** other Fairtrade items available in Irish shops.

_____

_____

_____

Activity 6 – Picture Perfect: Fairtrade Fortnight

Fairtrade has been described as 'the difference between life with and life without'. In the space below design a poster to promote Fairtrade Fortnight (first two weeks of March), outlining the benefits of Fairtrade to small producers in the Developing World. Don't forget to include a slogan and details of how people can get further information from Fairtrade Ireland.

Activity 7 - Exam Practice: Fairtrade

Look at the article below and answer the questions that follow.

A TASTE FOR LIFE

It takes a woman (tea pluckers are usually women) sixteen pluckings to pick enough tea for a single cup of tea. The delicate tea leaves are collected in woven baskets.

The daily wages of the pluckers depend on the amount of tea leaves they pick.
Unfortunately, as with many other products we buy from Third World producers, the prices paid to tea producers have not gone up in over forty years.

Tea pluckers receive a bonus for the tea sold under Fairtrade conditions. This bonus allows them to improve their housing, electricity and water supply.

Choose foods with the FAIRTRADE MARK: tea, coffee, chocolate, sugar, fresh fruit, juices, honey, biscuits and cereal bars.

Guarantees **a better deal** for Third World Producers

FAIRTRADE

Fairtrade Mark Ireland
Carmichael House.
North Brunswick Street. Dublin 7
01-475 3515 info@fairtrade.ie
www.fairtrade.ie

1 The article is about a campaign to do with trading fairly. Name the group organising the campaign. _____

   What does Fairtrade guarantee?
   _____
   (2 marks)

2 Give **ONE** reason why the wages of tea pluckers are so low.
   _____
   (2 marks)

3 Fairtrade tea pluckers get a bonus. Why is this very important to them?
   _____
   _____
   (4 marks)

4 Name **TWO** Fairtrade Mark foods that are available in Ireland.
   First Food _____
   Second Food_____
   (2 marks)

5 In March each year, Fairtrade Fortnight is held in Ireland to promote Fairtrade.
   Describe **TWO** actions your CSPE class could take to promote Fairtrade in your school as part of Fairtrade Fortnight.
   First Action _____
   Second Action _____
   (4 marks)

Adapted from Junior Certificate Exam

Activity 8 - Get Writing: Ethical Consumerism

Read the words of Mahatma Gandhi below. Explain how they relate to Fairtrade and your responsibilities as a consumer.

"Whenever you are in doubt, apply the following test: recall the face of the poorest and weakest person you may have seen and ask yourself if the step you contemplate is going to be of any use to them."

– Mahatma Gandhi

_____
_____
_____
_____
_____
_____
_____
_____
_____
_____
_____
_____
_____
_____
_____
_____
_____
_____
_____
_____
_____

Activity 9 - Picture Perfect: EU Member States

Look at the map of Europe below. Colour in the EU member states. Place a € sign on countries that have adopted the euro as their currency.

Activity 10 - Fill in the Gaps: The European Union

Take a look at the section on the EU in your textbook and fill in the blanks below.

The European Union is a group of twenty-seven states who work together to improve the lives of all their citizens. The EU used to be known as the EEC but changed its name after the **M**_____ Treaty. Ireland joined the group in **19**_____. Many EU members share a currency called the **E** _____. These notes and coins were introduced in **20** _____.

Governments of Europe are represented at the **C**_____ of the European Union. This allows heads of state and government ministers to meet and discuss policies.

Citizens of Europe are represented at the European **P**_____ by MEPs. Ireland has **T** _____ MEPs. All of Europe's MEPs meet in **S** _____ or Brussels to help govern Europe.

The European **C** _____ is sometimes considered the civil service of Europe. Its job is to make sure that policies are being implemented. Commissioners do not answer to their own countries but rather to the European Union itself.

Activity 11 – Exam Practice: Europe Day

Europe Day, 9 May

In 1985 9 May was chosen by the EU as the date on which to celebrate Europe Day. Your **CSPE** class has decided to celebrate Europe Day as part of your learning about interdependence.

1   Write a short speech for school assembly explaining your Europe Day programme of celebration. You should include a description of **THREE** different activities which everyone can take part in in order to learn more about the European Union.

_____

_____

_____

_____

_____

_____

_____

_____

_____

_____

_____

_____

(6 marks)

2   Apart from making a speech at the school assembly, describe **TWO** ways in which **YOUR CLASS** could raise awareness about your Europe Day celebrations.

_____

_____

_____

_____

_____

_____

_____

(6 marks)

3   Name and explain **TWO** skills that **YOU AND YOUR CLASSMATES** would use while raising awareness about your Europe Day celebrations.

_____

_____

_____

_____

_____

_____

_____

(8 marks)

Adapted from Junior Certificate Exam

Activity 12 - Go Find Out: Famous Faces

Find out who the current Secretary General of The United Nations is. Insert his/her picture from the internet or the newspaper. *Hint:* **go to www.un.org to get information.**

Secretary General of The United Nations
Name: _____

Go to www.europa.eu to find out who the following people are.

Ireland's EU Commissioner
Name: _____

An Irish MEP for your constituency
Name: _____

Activity 13 – Picture Perfect: The United Nations

The United Nations is involved in many different areas such as: Peacekeeping, Human Rights, World Health, International Economy, World Heritage Sites. Design a poster to represent all of these aspects of the United Nations.

OIDEACHAS SIBHIALTA, SÓISIALTA AGUS POLAITIÚIL
CIVIC, SOCIAL AND POLITICAL EDUCATION
TUAIRISC AR THIONSCADAL GNÍOMHAÍOCHTA
REPORT ON AN ACTION PROJECT

Scrúduimhir
Examination Number

Iarrtar ar iarrthóirí leathanaigh 1-11 sa fhreagarleabhar seo a léamh.
Candidates are asked to read pages 1 – 11 inclusive, in this answer book.

Ní mór do gach iarrthóir an Tuairisc a scríobh ina c(h)uid focal féin.
Each candidate must write the Report in his/her own words.

Don Scrúdaitheoir amháin For Examiner's use only

Roinn Section		An tUasmharc atá ar fáil Maximum mark available	An Marc a fuair an t-iarrthóir Mark received by candidate
1	**Mo Thionscadal Gníomhaíochta** My ActionProject	3 mharc/marks	
2	**Réamhrá** **Introduction** (a) Identification and explanation of concept *An coincheap a shonrú agus a mhíniú* (b) One other reason *Cúis amháin eile*	4 mharc/marks 4 mharc/marks	
3	**Gníomhaíochtaí a rinneadh** **Activities Undertaken** (a) Type of action and communication with people *An cineál gníomhaíochta agus cumarsáide le daoine* (b) List and description of activities *Liosta gníomhaíochtaí agus cuntas orthu* (c) Detailed account of one activity *Mionchuntas ar ghníomhaíocht amháin* (d) Application of skills *Cur i bhfeidhm scileanna*	4 mharc/marks 15 mharc/marks 15 mharc/marks 15 mharc/marks	
4	Achoimre ar an eolas Summary of information	30 marc/marks	
5	Smaointe Reflections	30 marc/marks	
	Iomlán	120 marc/marks	
	Total	Iomlán bun leathanaigh End of page Total	

ROINN 1. Mo Thionscadal Gníomhaíochta
SECTION 1. My Action Project

Teideal mo Thionscadail Ghníomhaíochta
The Title of my Action Project

_____

_____

Cuir tic ✓ le do thoil leis an gcineál / na cineálacha gníomhaíochta a rinneadh mar chuid den Tionscadal Gníomhaíochta.
Please tick ✓ the type/s of action that was/were undertaken as part of the Action Project

Suirbhé/Ceistneoir Survey/Questionnaire ☐	Agallamh Interview ☐	Foilseachán Publication ☐
Forbairt Tuisceana Awareness raising ☐	Feachtas Campaign ☐	Lá Ainmnithe Designated day ☐
Aoichainteoir Guest speaker ☐	Bréagthoghchán/ parlaimint Mock election/ parliament ☐	Bailiú airgid Fundraising ☐
Fiosrúchán Investigation ☐	Cuairt Visit ☐	Gníomhaíocht Chomhairle Daltaí Student Council activity ☐

Eile (tabhair cuntas le do thoil ar an gcineál gníomhaíochta)
Other (please describe the type of action undertaken)

_____

_____

ROINN 2. Réamhrá   **(3 mharc/marks)**
SECTION 2. Introduction

(a)   **Cuir tic ✓ le do thoil le coincheap AMHÁIN a raibh do Thionscadal Gníomhaíochta bunaithe air.**
     Please tick ✓ ONE concept on which your Action Project was based.

An Daonlathas Democracy ☐	Cearta agus Freagrachtaí Rights and Responsibilities ☐
Dínit an Duine Human Dignity ☐	An tIdirspleáchas Interdependence ☐
An Fhorbairt Development ☐	An Mhaoirseacht An Dlí Stewardship ☐ Law ☐

Mínigh an chaoi a raibh do Thionscadal Gníomhaíochta bunaithe ar an gcoincheap ar chuir tú tic leis.
Explain how your Action Project was based on the concept you have ticked.

_____

_____

_____

_____

                                         (4 mharc/marks)

Don Oifig Amháin
Office use only

Scr./Comh. Ex./Adv.	Scr. Ach App. Ex

(b) Mínigh cén fáth ar roghnaigh tú an Tionscadal Gníomhaíochta seo a dhéanamh.
Explain why you chose to do this Action Project.

_____
_____
_____
_____
_____
_____
_____
_____
_____

(4 mharc/marks)

ROINN 3. Gníomhaíochtaí a rinneadh
SECTION 3. Activities undertaken

(a) Liostaigh BEIRT nó DHÁ ghrúpa a raibh tú i gcumarsáid leo le linn do Thionscadail Ghníomhaíochta
List <u>TWO</u> people/groups you communitcted with in the course of your Action Project

1ú duine / grúpa
1st person / group

_____
_____

2ú duine / grúpa
2nd person / group _____
_____

Déan cur síos ar an gCAOI a ndearna tú cumarsáid le duine / grúpa amháin díobh sin a liostaigh tú thuas agus mínigh CÉN FÁTH a ndearna tú é.
Describe HOW you communicated with ONE of the people / groups you have listed above, and explain WHY you did so.

_____
_____
_____
_____
_____
_____
_____

(4 mharc/marks)

(b) Scríobh liosta de na príomhthascanna/príomhghníomhaíochtaí a rinneadh mar chuid den Tionscadal Gníomhaíochta agus déan cur síos gairid orthu.

Write a list and brief description of the main tasks/activities undertaken as part of your Action Project

_____

_____

_____

_____

_____

_____

_____

_____

_____

_____

_____

_____

_____

_____

_____

_____

_____

_____

_____

_____

_____

_____

_____

_____

_____

_____

_____

Don Oifig Amháin
Office use only

Scr./Comh. Ex./Adv.	Scr. Ach App. Ex

(15 mharc/marks)

(c) Tabhair mionchuntas ar thasc/ghníomhaíocht **AMHÁIN** ar leith ón liosta i Roinn (B) a rinne **TUSA** mar chuid de do Thionscadal Gníomhaíochta.

Give a detailed account of **ONE** particular task/activity from the list in Section (b) that **YOU** undertook as part of your Action Project.

Don Oifig Amháin
Office use only

Scr./Comh. Ex./Adv.	Scr. Ach App. Ex

_____

_____

_____

_____

_____

_____

_____

_____

_____

_____

_____

_____

_____

_____

_____

_____

_____

_____

_____

_____

_____

_____

_____

_____

_____

_____

_____

_____

(15 mharc/marks)

(d) Ainmnigh DHÁ scil a d'úsáid tú agus tú ag déanamh na gníomhaíochta ar thug tú cuntas air i gcuid (c) agus déan cur síos ar an gcaoi ar úsáid tú an DÁ scil.

Name **TWO** skills that you used when undertaking the activity you have given an account of in part (c) and describe how yo used these **TWO** skills.

An Chéad Scil / First Skill _____

Cur Síos / Description _____

_____

_____

_____

_____

_____

_____

An Dara Scil / Second Skill _____

Cur Síos / Description _____

_____

_____

_____

_____

_____

_____

_____

Mínigh cén fáth a raibh ceann AMHÁIN de na scileanna sin tábhachtach agus tú ag déanamh do Thionscadail Ghníomhaíochta. Explain why ONE of these skills was important in carrying out your Action Project.

Míniú / Description _____

_____

_____

_____

_____

_____

_____

                                                              (15 mharc/marks)

ROINN 4. Achoimre ar an eolas a d'fhoghlaim tú
SECTION 4. Summary of information learned

Don Oifig Amháin
Office use only

Scr./Comh. Ex./Adv.	Scr. Ach App. Ex

D'fhoghlaim tú a lán rudaí éagsúla le linn do Thionscadail Ghníomhaíochta.

Déan achoimre ar an méid a d'fhoghlaim tú. Déan cinnte de go dtugann tú mionchuntas ar CHÚIG mhír eolais éagsúla a d'fhoghlaim tú.

During the course of your Action Project you will have learned many different things. Give a summary of your learning making sure to write in detail about at least FIVE different pieces of in formation that you acquired.

_____
_____
_____
_____
_____
_____
_____
_____
_____
_____
_____
_____
_____
_____
_____
_____
_____
_____
_____
_____
_____
_____
_____
_____
_____

(30 mharc/marks)

ROINN 5. SMAOINTE
SECTION 5. Reflections

Caith súil siar ar na heispéiris éagsúla a bhí agat agus tú i mbun do Thionscadail Ghníomhaíochta. Luaigh cúiseanna ar chabhraigh na heispéiris sin chun do chuid smaointe agus tuairimí a mhúnlú.

Think back on the different experiences you had while doing your Action Project.
Give reasons why these experiences helped to shape your thoughts and opinions.

_____

_____

_____

_____

_____

_____

_____

_____

_____

_____

_____

_____

_____

_____

_____

_____

_____

_____

_____

_____

_____

_____

_____

_____

_____

**Don Oifig Amháin
Office use only**

Scr./Comh. Ex./Adv.	Scr. Ach App. Ex

(30 mharc/marks)

Thionscadal Gníomhaíochta an Dalta - Riachtanais
Student Action Project Requirements

☐ Ba chóir go mbeadh an Tionscadal Gníomhaíochta bunaithe go soiléir ar cheann amháin nó níos mó de na seacht gcoincheap ar an gcúrsa
The Action Project should be clearly based on one or more of the seven course concepts.

☐ Ba chóir go mbeadh an coincheap ag teacht leis an bpeirspictíocht ar chearta daonna agus ar an bhfreagracht shóisialta san Oideachas Sibhialta, Sóisialta agus Polaitiúil.
The Action should be consistent with the human rights and social responsibility perspective of Civic, Social and Political Education.

☐ Ba chóir go mbeadh gné ghníomhaíochta ag baint leis an Tionscadal Tíomhaíochta.
The Action Project should have an action component.

☐ Ba chóir go gcuirfeadh an Tionscadal Gníomhaíochta ar chumas an dalta dul ag plé/i mbun cumarsáide le daoine nó le pobail eile faoi ábhar na gníomhaíochta.
The Action Project should enable the student to engage/communicate with other people or communities about the subject of their action.

☐ Ba chóir go gcuirfeadh an Tionscadal Gníomhaíochta ar chumas an dalta na scileanna a bhaineann leis an Oideachas Sibhialta, Sóisialta agus Polaitiúil a chleachtadh.
The Action Project should enable the student to practice the skills associated with Civic, Social and Political Education.

☐ Ba chóir go gcuirfeadh an Tionscadal Gníomhaíochta ar chumas an dalta a c(h)uid eolais agus tuisceana ar ábhar na gníomhaíochta a fhorbairt.
The Action Project should enable the student to develop his/her knowledge and understanding of the subject of the action.

☐ Ba chóir go mbeadh gné mhachnaimh agus luachála san áireamh sa Tionscadal Gníomhaíochta.
The Action Project should include a reflection and evaluation dimension.

Blank Page
Leathanach Bán